He used **MIRROR WRITING** — he wrote from right to left!

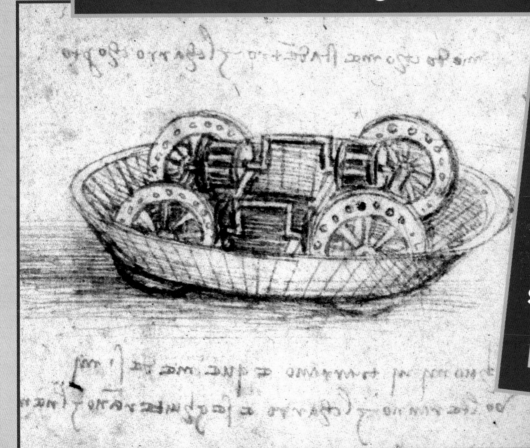

To keep people from stealing his ideas? To keep the ink from smearing? **NO ONE KNOWS.**

3

X-RAYS

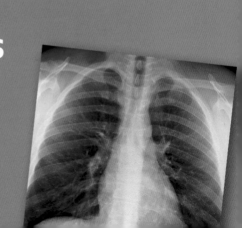

1895, WILHELM CONRAD ROENTGEN

One of the **FIRST X-RAYS** was of Roentgen's wife's **HAND**. You can **SEE** her wedding ring!

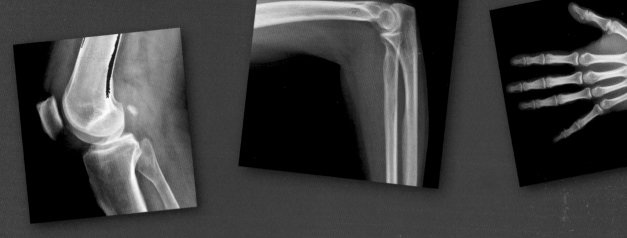

The "X" **IN X-RAYS** comes from maths, where "X" equals **"UNKNOWN"**. At first Roentgen didn't know where the strange ray came from.

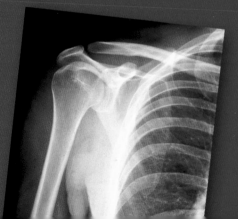

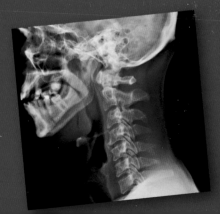

GALILEO

(1564-1642)

With his **TELESCOPE** Galileo discovered four of Jupiter's **MOONS**.

HE PROVED COPERNICUS' IDEA THAT THE PLANETS GO AROUND THE SUN.

He also invented the first **PENDULUM CLOCK.** But he never quite finished it.

WHEEL

The **FIRST WHEEL** was invented around 3500 BC. It was used to **MAKE POTTERY**.

THREE HUNDRED YEARS LATER, WHEELS WERE PUT ON CARTS.

The first wheels in North America were used on CHILDREN'S TOYS.

FRANK ZAMBONI

(1901-1988)

In 1953 Zamboni patented the first "ICE RESURFACER".

HIS COMPANY ALSO INVENTED

THE GRASSHOPPER – a machine that ROLLS OUT Astroturf™

THE BLACK WIDOW – a machine that puts SOIL ON TOP of graves

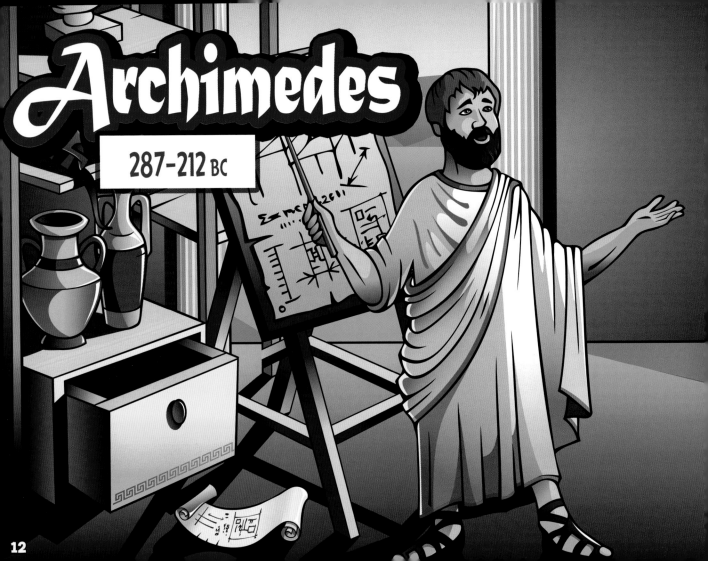

Archimedes

287–212 BC

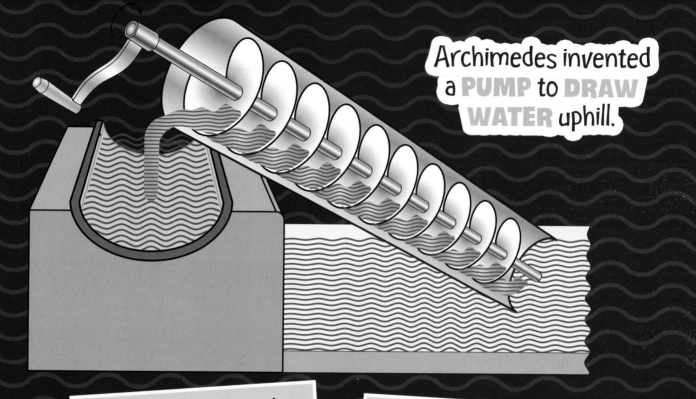

Archimedes invented a **PUMP** to **DRAW WATER** uphill.

He also invented the **"ARCHIMEDES CLAW"** - a **HUGE HOOK** that could flip enemy ships.

His **"HEAT RAY"** was a set of **GIANT MIRRORS**. When enemy ships came near, the mirrors were angled to shine sunlight at the ships.

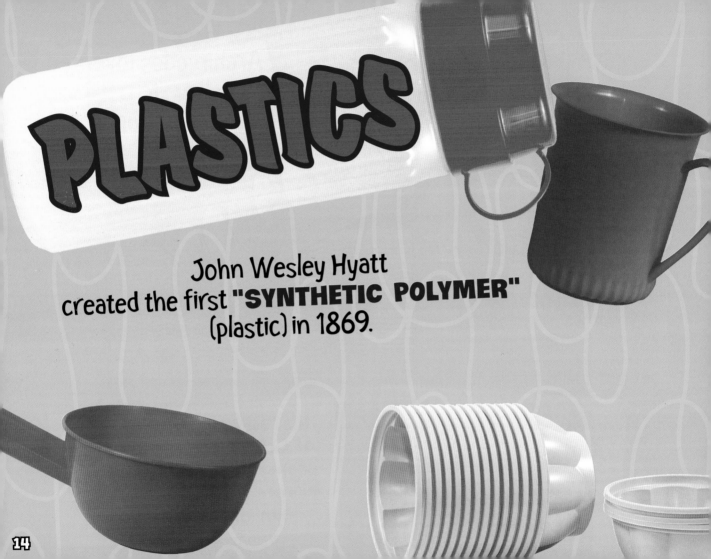

PLASTICS

John Wesley Hyatt created the first **"SYNTHETIC POLYMER"** (plastic) in 1869.

The word "plastic" comes from the **LATIN** word "plasticus" and the **GREEK** word "plastikos". The words mean **BEING ABLE TO BE MOULDED**.

FLEECE is a fabric made from **RECYCLED** plastic bottles.

SUBMARINE

The first working submarine was a **ROWING BOAT** covered in **LEATHER.**

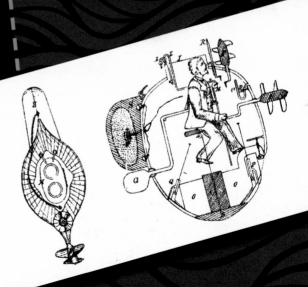

THE TURTLE was the first submarine used in battle. It was meant to **ATTACH BOMBS** to ships, but it **FAILED**.

How deep do today's military subs go? That's **CLASSIFIED** information!

LEGO

1932,
OLE KIRCH CHRISTIANSEN

The LEGO moulds are **VERY EXACT.** Only about **18 IN 1 MILLION** pieces are thrown away for poor quality.

More than 4 billion **LEGO PEOPLE** have been made. That's **THREE TIMES** the population of China!

The **VERY FIRST** LEGO piece was made of **WOOD**.

BENJAMIN FRANKLIN

Franklin's inventions include **BIFOCALS** and the **ROCKING CHAIR**. He also invented the **FRANKLIN STOVE** and the **LIGHTNING ROD**.

He stopped going to school at **AGE 10**.

He almost **DIED** while trying to heal a **PARALYSED** man by **ELECTROCUTING** him.

He **TAUGHT HIMSELF** French, Italian, Latin and Spanish.

TELEVISION

In 1884 Paul Nipkow invented a disk that broke images into **POINTS** and **LINES**. John Logie Baird later used it to make a **MECHANICAL TELEVISION**. His TV's first image, in 1925, was of a **VENTRILOQUIST'S DUMMY**.

The first TV program shown **IN COLOUR** in the United States was the 1954 Tournament of Roses Parade.

The first **REMOTE CONTROL** (1950) was connected to the television set with a wire.

ROCKET

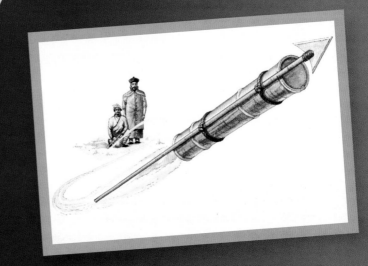

The Chinese were the **FIRST PEOPLE** to use rockets. They used them for **FIREWORKS**.

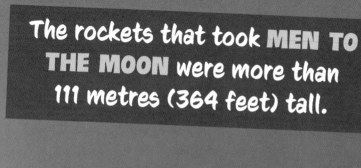

The rockets that took **MEN TO THE MOON** were more than 111 metres (364 feet) tall.

A space shuttle's solid rocket boosters could go to **FULL POWER** in only two-tenths of a second. It takes longer to **BLINK YOUR EYES**! (NASA's space shuttle program ended in 2011.)

PAPER

2,000+ YEARS AGO, TS"AI LUN

Lun's paper was made from **MULBERRY BUSH FIBRES**. Later, fishing nets and rags were added. The materials were **COOKED, BEATEN** into a **PASTE** and **DRIED**.

BEFORE PAPER, PEOPLE WROTE ON BAMBOO, WOOD, CLAY AND ANIMAL SKINS.

BICYCLE

1818

THE FIRST BICYCLE DID NOT HAVE PEDALS.

"**BONESHAKERS**" was the name given to early bikes. Why? They really **RATTLED**!

In 2008 Phil Bridge invented a **BICYCLE** made of cardboard. Everything except the wheel rims, tyres and crankset were made of **CARDBOARD**.

THE
FLUSH
TOILET

1596,
SIR JOHN HARINGTON

TODAY'S TOILETS

USE UP TO **6.1 LITRES (1.6 GALLONS)** OF WATER PER FLUSH. UNTIL THE MID-1990S, THEY USED UP TO **26.5 LITRES (7 GALLONS)**.

A Japanese company makes a toilet that **CLEANS ITSELF** and cleans (and dries) **YOU!** It opens and closes the lid by itself. It also has a **HEATED SEAT, SOUND SYSTEM, AIR FRESHENER** and **NIGHT-LIGHT!**

BOARD GAME

One of the world's **FIRST BOARD GAMES** was **SENET**. The ancient Egyptian game dated back to around 3100 BC. Players threw **STICKS** like dice and moved pieces from square to square.

VAIKUNTAPAALI, the basis for **SNAKES AND LADDERS**, was invented in India in the 1500s.

What's the most **POPULAR** board game ever? Probably **CHESS**.

33

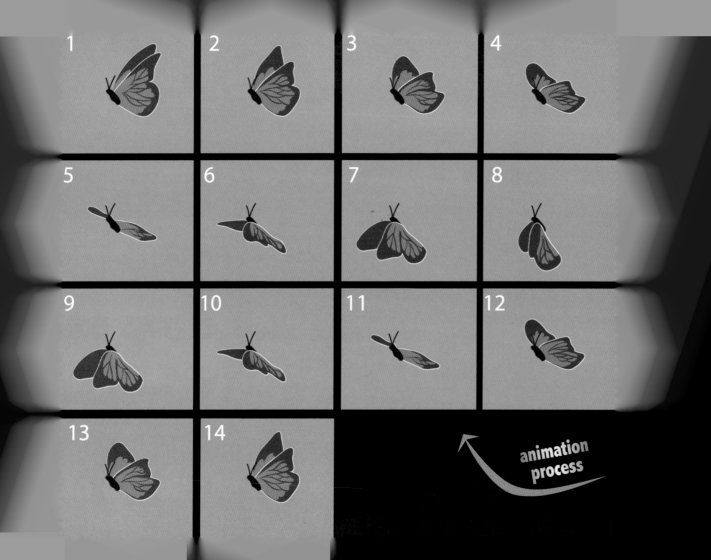

animation process

animation

The animation process is SLOW. It takes SEVERAL MONTHS to make ONE 30-MINUTE SHOW.

Many early CARTOON CHARACTERS had only FOUR fingers. They were easier to draw that way.

The Apostle (1917) was the FIRST ANIMATED feature film. No copies exist today.

TOY STORY (1995) was the first feature film animated ENTIRELY BY COMPUTER.

internet

THERE WAS NOT ONE "INVENTOR" OF THE INTERNET.

IT CAME TOGETHER FROM MANY IDEAS AND TECHNOLOGIES.

TIM BERNERS-LEE

INVENTED THE WORLD WIDE WEB (HTTP:\\) in 1989.
It made the internet free for all.

One **Google** query
takes **1,000** computers
0.2 SECONDS
to get an answer.

SMALLPOX VACCINATION

1796, EDWARD JENNER

THE SMALLPOX VACCINE WAS THE FIRST VACCINE IN THE WORLD.

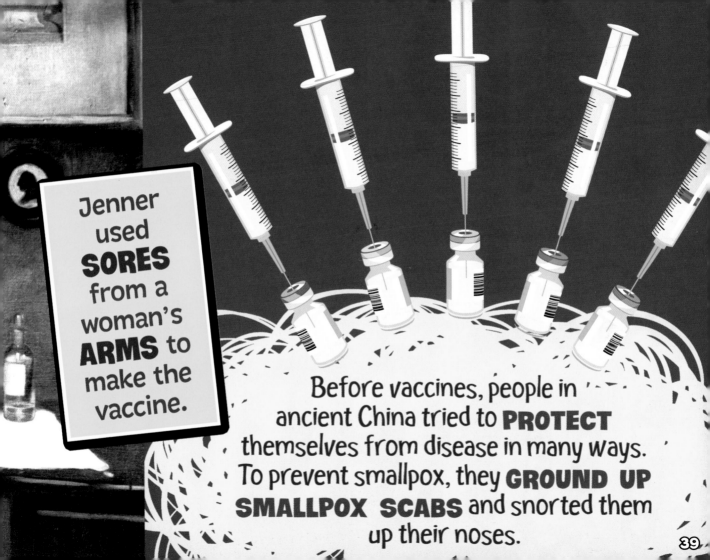

Jenner used **SORES** from a woman's **ARMS** to make the vaccine.

Before vaccines, people in ancient China tried to **PROTECT** themselves from disease in many ways. To prevent smallpox, they **GROUND UP SMALLPOX SCABS** and snorted them up their noses.

39

BIZARRE INVENTION

Unicorn

1984, TIMOTHY G ZELL

TO "MAKE" **UNICORNS,** HE PERFORMED SURGERY ON THE HORN BUDS ON WHITE BABY GOATS.

Some of the "unicorns" were sold to **RINGLING BROS. and BARNUM & BAILEY CIRCUS.**

TAPEWORM TRAP

1854, Dr. Alpheus Myers

HERE'S HOW IT WORKED:

1) Patient doesn't eat for several days.

2) Patient swallows baited trap attached to string.

3) Tapeworm finds bait.

4) Trap shuts and grabs the tapeworm's head.

5) Patient pulls on string, and trap and tapeworm come up out of patient's mouth.

43

BIZARRE INVENTION

BABY CAGE

1922, EMMA READ

THE IDEA?

Babies who live in apartments
need fresh air and sun too!

The wire cage **HUNG ON THE SIDE** of a
building, outside an **OPEN WINDOW**. It had
a roof to protect babies from rain and snow.

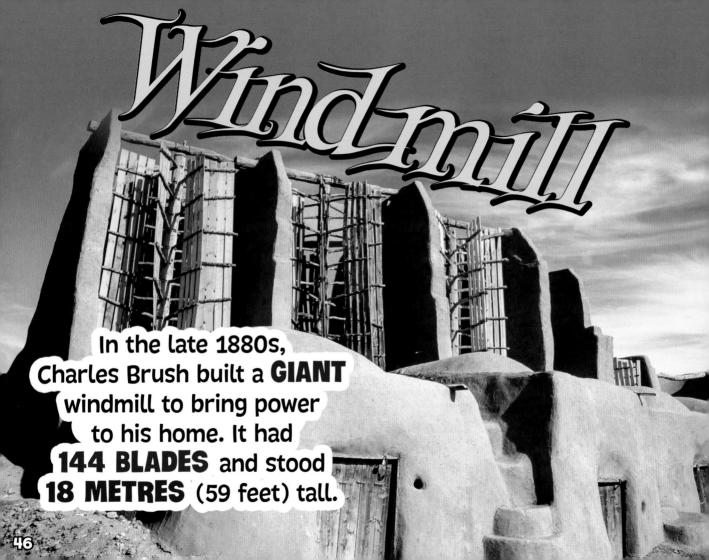

Windmill

In the late 1880s, Charles Brush built a **GIANT** windmill to bring power to his home. It had **144 BLADES** and stood **18 METRES** (59 feet) tall.

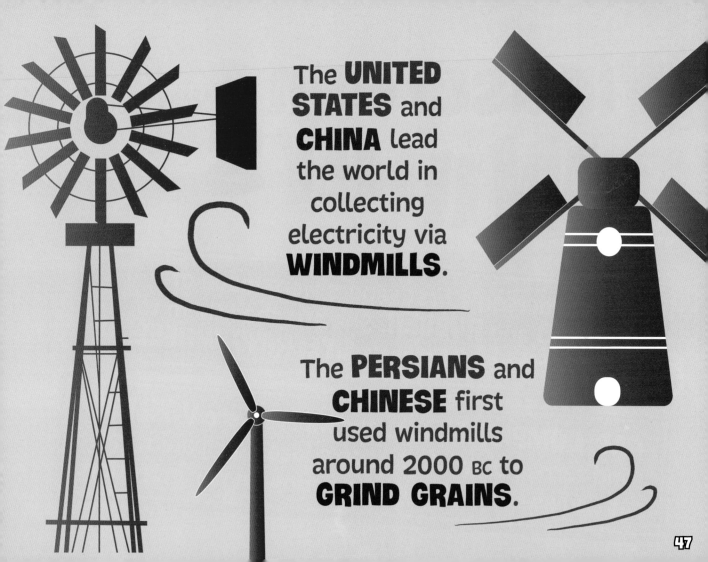

The **UNITED STATES** and **CHINA** lead the world in collecting electricity via **WINDMILLS**.

The **PERSIANS** and **CHINESE** first used windmills around 2000 BC to **GRIND GRAINS**.

47

Windscreen Wipers

Anderson's first wipers were made of **WOOD** and **RUBBER**. She attached them to a **LEVER** near the car's **STEERING WHEEL**.

CAR COMPANIES thought wipers were **USELESS** and turned down Anderson's idea. Her patent ran out and she **NEVER** made a penny on her invention.

48

WINDSCREEN WIPERS WERE STANDARD ON CARS 10 YEARS LATER.

GLASSES AND CONTACT LENSES

Sometime in the late 1200s,
glasses appeared in Italy.
NO ONE IS SURE WHO INVENTED THEM.

The **FIRST** contact lenses were **MADE OF GLASS!**
HARD PLASTIC contact lenses were
INVENTED in 1936.

SOFT CONTACTS were invented in 1971.
They were made of flexible,
WATER-ABSORBING plastic.

WRIGHT BROTHERS

(Wilbur 1867–1912, Orville 1871–1948)

THE WRIGHT BROTHERS' FIRST FLIGHT, IN 1903, LASTED ONLY 12 SECONDS.

ORVILLE was the first to **FLY** the aeroplane. He won a **COIN TOSS**.

NEIL ARMSTRONG carried pieces of the Wright Flyer with him to the **MOON** in 1969.

AEROPLANE

The **FASTEST** manned aircraft **EVER RECORDED** – the X-15 – went mach 6.7. That's about **7,200 KILOMETRES** (4,474 miles) per hour!

The **LARGEST** passenger aeroplane in the world is the Airbus A380. It can carry **853 PEOPLE**.

VENDING MACHINE

2,000 YEARS AGO, HERO OF ALEXANDRIA

The **FIRST** vending machine gave out **HOLY WATER.**

In 1883 Percival Everitt **INVENTED** a machine that gave out **POSTCARDS.**

In China you can buy **LIVE CRABS** from a vending machine.

Jerome Lemelson

(1923-1997)

Patents

Clients

Lemelson was **ALWAYS INVENTING**. He received a **PATENT** each month for more than **40 YEARS!**

He kept a **NOTEBOOK** by his bed to record ideas from his **DREAMS.**

HE INVENTED HUNDREDS AND HUNDREDS OF THINGS, FROM TALKING THERMOMETERS TO ROBOTS.

ICE CREAM

The **FIRST ICE CREAM** was likely invented by the **CHINESE** more than 1,300 years ago. But iced desserts were around **LONG BEFORE** that.

The first ice-cream **CONE** showed up about **115 YEARS** ago.

Today's food **SCIENTISTS** invent all kinds of bizarre ice creams, including **"MELTLESS"** ice cream.

61

THE ISOLATOR

1925, HUGO GERNSBACK

DO YOU HAVE TROUBLE CONCENTRATING? Get yourself an ISOLATOR!

ZARRE VENTION

Dimple Maker

1936,
ISABELLA GILBERT

BORN
WITHOUT
DIMPLES?

NO
PROBLEM.

USE THE
DIMPLE
MAKER!

A spring with two **SMALL KNOBS** fit over a person's face. The knobs **PRESSED** into the cheeks.

Did it work? **Not really.**

65

THOMAS EDISON

1847–1931

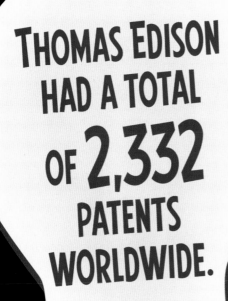

THOMAS EDISON HAD A TOTAL OF 2,332 PATENTS WORLDWIDE.

As a boy, Edison wanted to know why **GEESE** sat on their eggs. To find out, he sat on a nest of eggs for **HOURS**.

THOMAS EDISON

HE INVENTED THOUSANDS OF THINGS:

the phonograph, the universal electric motor, the incandescent light bulb, the film camera and more.

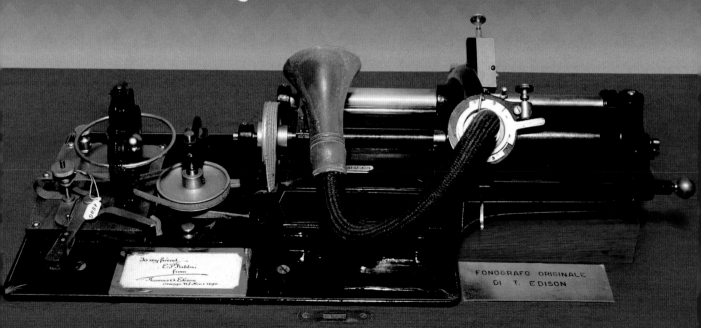

THE FIRST MESSAGE RECORDED ON EDISON'S PHONOGRAPH WAS "Mary had a little lamb".

3D BIOPRINTER
Desktop Printer

THE 3D BIOPRINTER CAN MAKE MINI HUMAN ORGANS.

It uses a **SPECIAL INK** that is mixed with **LIVING CELLS.**

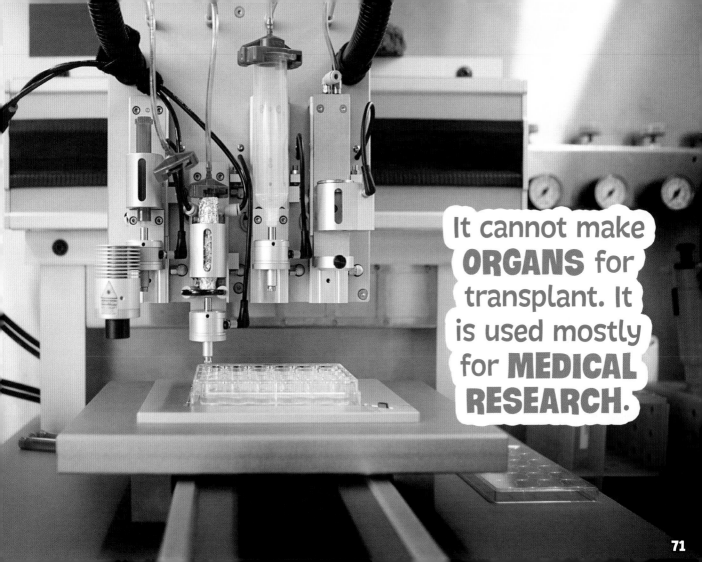

It cannot make **ORGANS** for transplant. It is used mostly for **MEDICAL RESEARCH.**

BALLOON

The **EARLIEST** balloons were made from **ANIMAL BLADDERS** and other animal parts.

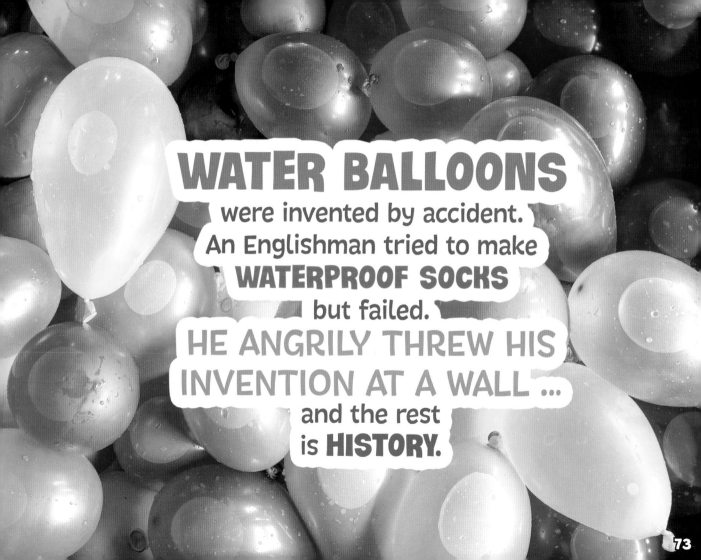

WATER BALLOONS were invented by accident. An Englishman tried to make **WATERPROOF SOCKS** but failed. **HE ANGRILY THREW HIS INVENTION AT A WALL** ... and the rest is **HISTORY**.

ELEVATOR

Simple **ROPE-PULLED** elevators were first used in 236 BC. They were very **DANGEROUS**. Ropes often broke!

In 1853 **ELISHA OTIS** came up with a **SAFETY BRAKE** for elevators. From then on, elevators became **WIDELY USED.**

SOON SOME ELEVATORS WILL GO SIDEWAYS!

Microwave OVEN

THE MICROWAVE OVEN WAS INVENTED BY ACCIDENT DURING WORLD WAR II.

Percy Lebaron Spencer was using a **RADAR**, when he noticed his **CHOCOLATE** had melted nearby. The radar worked by using **MICRO WAVES**. This discovery led to cooking foods with micro waves.

The **FIRST MICROWAVE OVEN** weighed about **340 KILOGRAMS** (750 pounds). It stood nearly **1.8 METRES** (6 feet) tall.

Chocolate was invented more than **4,000** years ago in **SOUTH AMERICA.**

The **FIRST CHOCOLATE** was a **DRINK**, not a food.

The first **CHOCOLATE BAR** wasn't created until 1847.

JEANS

1873, Levi Strauss and Jacob Davis

JEANS WERE FIRST INVENTED AS STURDY WORK TROUSERS FOR MINERS.

RIVETS were put in jeans so the **SEAMS** did not tear.

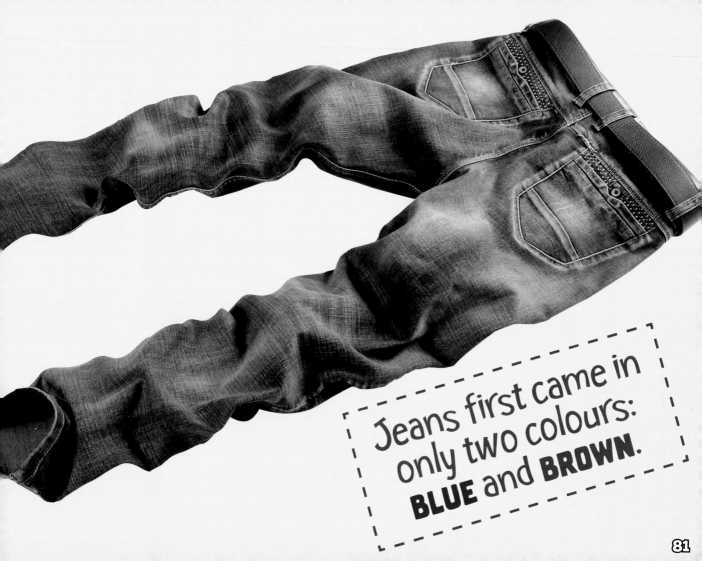

Jeans first came in only two colours: **BLUE** and **BROWN**.

SATELLITE

THE SOVIET UNION PUT THE FIRST SATELLITE, *SPUTNIK*, INTO ORBIT IN 1957.

Today there are more than **4,000 ARTIFICIAL SATELLITES** orbiting Earth.

SPUTNIK
WAS THE
SIZE OF A
BEACH BALL.

Washing Machine

Before **WASHING MACHINES**, people spent hours washing clothes **BY HAND**. They beat clothing against **ROCKS** to clean it.

People later rubbed their clothes against **RIBBED METAL BOARDS** called washboards.

In 1851 James King patented the first **"DRUM"** washing machine. It was bulky and **CRANKED BY HAND**, but it saved time.

ARTIFICIAL BODY PARTS

ANCIENT EGYPTIANS replaced certain body parts, such as **HANDS** and **FEET**, with **WOOD**.

In France during the 1500s, Ambroise Paré invented an **ARTIFICIAL HAND**. Springs allowed the fingers to **FLEX**.

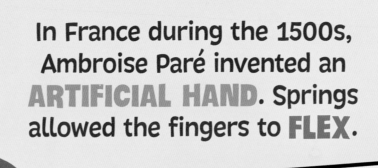

Today's artificial limbs can look just like **NATURAL** limbs. Some may include hair, nails and even **FRECKLES**!

Scientists are working on **CREATING LIMBS** that can be controlled by a person's **THOUGHTS**.

Camera

The earliest cameras were **BIG AND CLUNKY**. Models had to sit **TOTALLY STILL** for one to three minutes or the photos **BLURRED**.

The first camera **WIDELY USED** by the public was the **BROWNIE.** It came out in 1900 and cost 80p.

THE POLAROID, or instant picture camera, went on sale in 1948. The camera held **SPECIAL PAPER** and **CHEMICALS INSIDE.** Photos could be taken and **PRINTED** on the spot within 60 seconds.

Cristofori was a **HARPSICHORD MAKER**. He wanted to build a similar instrument that could be played softly or loudly to create **DIFFERENT MOODS**.

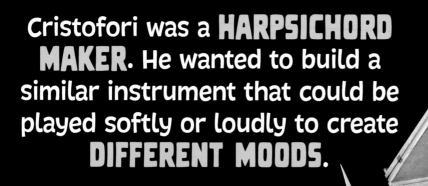

The harpsichord was invented before the piano. But it could be played at only one volume.

WHITE PIANO KEYS were originally made from **ELEPHANT TUSKS**. **BLACK KEYS** were made of tropical tree wood called **EBONY**.

CRAYONS

"Modern" **crayons** first appeared in Europe. They were made of **charcoal** and **oil**.

CRAYOLA Crayons were first sold in 1903.

Crayola makes nearly **3 BILLION** crayons per year – in **120 DIFFERENT COLOURS**!

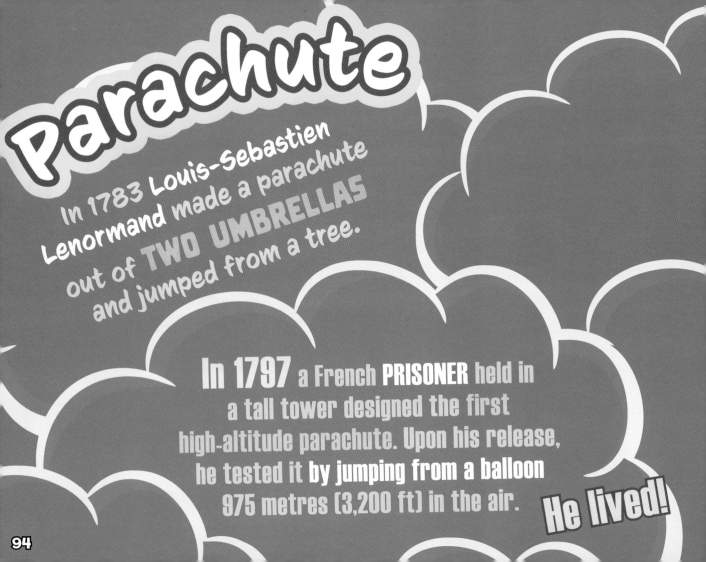

Parachute

In 1783 Louis-Sebastien Lenormand made a parachute out of **TWO UMBRELLAS** and jumped from a tree.

In 1797 a French **PRISONER** held in a tall tower designed the first high-altitude parachute. Upon his release, he tested it **by jumping from a balloon** 975 metres (3,200 ft) in the air.

He lived!

Leonardo da Vinci's 1400s parachute design was tested in 2000. **IT WORKED!** And it had a smoother ride than today's parachutes.

SKATEBOARD

In the 1950s, the **FIRST SKATEBOARD** was made by attaching roller-skate wheels to a board.

Hermosa Beach, California, was the site of the **FIRST skateboarding CONTEST** in 1963.

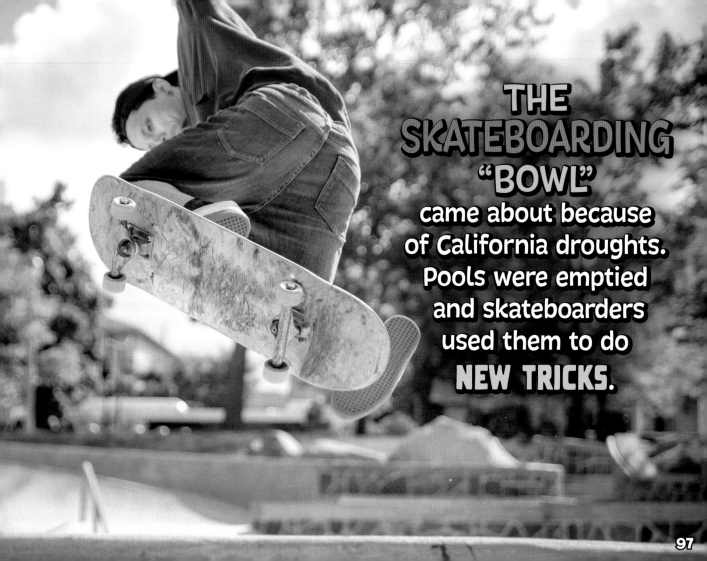

THE SKATEBOARDING "BOWL"

came about because of California droughts. Pools were emptied and skateboarders used them to do **NEW TRICKS**.

Let's Compare
THEN & NOW

COMPUTERS

In 1837 Charles Babbage built an early computer called the "ANALYTICAL MACHINE".

Early computers were **so big** that they filled entire rooms!

Today's **SMARTPHONES** 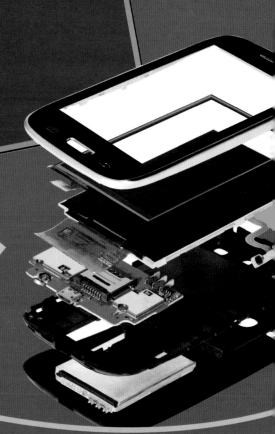 have more processing power than those large computers.

EXPERTS SAY THAT COMPUTERS MAY SOON BE PUT **INSIDE YOUR BODY.**

Let's Compare
THEN & NOW

CARS

The first car (1769) was powered by a **STEAM ENGINE**. It didn't go very fast – about 4 kilometres (2.5 miles) per hour!

HENRY FORD'S Model T (1908–1927) could go up to **72 KILOMETRES** (45 miles) per hour.

Although the MINI Cooper S is tiny, it can go up to 235 kilometres (146 miles) per hour.

In 2014 the HENNESSEY VENOM GT reached a speed of 435.3 kilometres (270.5 miles) per hour.

TOOTHBRUSHES

THE FIRST TOOTHBRUSHES WERE CALLED **"CHEW STICKS"**. THEY WERE SIMPLY STICKS WITH FRAYED ENDS.

The Chinese invented a **BRISTLED TOOTHBRUSH** in 1498. The bristles were hog hairs.

Today's **SONIC TOOTHBRUSH BRISTLES** move at about 30,000 to 40,000 strokes per minute.

GEORGE
WASHINGTON
CARVER

1864-1943

Contrary to popular belief, George Washington Carver did **NOT** invent peanut butter. The Aztecs and Incas were the **FIRST KNOWN PEOPLES** to mash up peanuts into a paste and spread it on food.

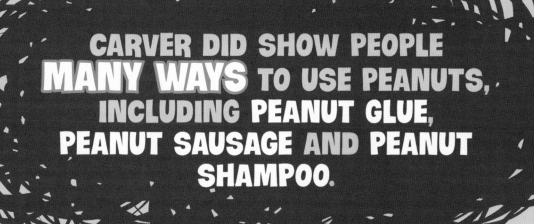

CARVER DID SHOW PEOPLE **MANY WAYS** TO USE PEANUTS, INCLUDING **PEANUT GLUE**, **PEANUT SAUSAGE** AND **PEANUT SHAMPOO.**

TELEPHONES

ALEXANDER GRAHAM BELL is widely thought to be the **INVENTOR** of the telephone. He made his first call in 1876.

THE FIRST MOBILE PHONE WAS SO BIG THAT IT NEEDED ITS OWN CARRYING BAG.

MATTI MAKKONEN invented the idea for **TEXTING** in 1984.

The **RUSSIANS** invented the roller coaster in the **1600s**.

ROLLER COASTERS

The **FIRST AMERICAN ROLLER COASTER** opened to the public in 1884. It went just **10 KILOMETRES** (6 miles) **PER HOUR!**

The **WORLD'S FASTEST** roller coaster is the Formula Rossa in the United Arab Emirates. It zooms at **240 KILOMETRES** (149 miles) **PER HOUR!**

GLOSSARY

altitude height of an object above sea level or ground level

artificial made by people

Aztec member of a group of Indian people who lived in Mexico before Spanish people settled there

classified top secret

drought long period of weather with little or no rainfall

electrocute pass electricity through a body, resulting in injury or death

harpsichord early keyboard instrument

holy water water that has been blessed by a church official

Inca member of a group of Indian people in South America

isolate cause a person or place to remain alone or apart from others

paralysed unable to move

patent get an official paper that gives a person the right to be the only one who makes something; a patent protects the person from other people stealing their ideas

pendulum stick that has a weight at the bottom that swings back and forth

radar device that uses radio waves to track the location of objects

rivet metal bolt used to hold things together

satellite spacecraft that circles Earth; satellites gather and send information to Earth

synthetic something made by combining different things

tapeworm long, ribbon-like flatworm that can live inside the intestines of humans and other animals

vaccine injection of medicine that prevents a disease

ventriloquist entertainer who makes their voice appear to come from a dummy of a person or animal

FIND OUT MORE

125 Cool Inventions, National Geographic Kids (National Geographic Kids, 2015)

100 Inventions That Made History, Tracey Turner, Andrea Mills and Clive Gifford (DK Publishing, 2014)

Oh, The Things They Invented!: All About Great Inventors, Bonnie Worth (Random House Books for Young Readers, 2015)

WEBSITES

http://inventorsproject.co.uk/inventions/

Find out more about a project where children had their designs made into real inventions.

http://www.dkfindout.com/uk/science/famous-scientists/

Learn more about famous inventors and scientists from around the world.

INDEX

Raintree is an imprint of Capstone Global Library Limited, a company incorporated in England and Wales
having its registered office at 264 Banbury Road, Oxford, OX2 7DY – Registered company number: 6695582

www.raintree.co.uk
myorders@raintree.co.uk

Text © Capstone Global Library Limited 2017
The moral rights of the proprietor have been asserted.

Edited by Jill Kalz and Megan Peterson
Picture research by Jo Miller

Designed by Veronica Scott
Production by Tori Abraham

Printed and bound in India

ISBN 978 1 4747 3740 1 (hardback)
21 20 19 18 17
10 9 8 7 6 5 4 3 2 1

ISBN 978 1 4747 3742 5 (paperback)
22 21 20 19 18
10 9 8 7 6 5 4 3 2 1

British Library Cataloguing in Publication Data
A full catalogue record for this book is available from the British Library.

Acknowledgements
Alamy: INTERFOTO, 23, Mirrorpix/Trinity Mirror, 40-41; Getty Images: Alireza Firouzi, 46 (all), Bettmann, 20, 38, 62, 63, 65,
GraphicaArtis, 3, N Smith, 45, Pictorial Parade, 77, The Print Collector, 27; Library of Congress, 53; MCT via Getty Images,
83; NASA, 6; Newscom: akg-images, 98, BSIP, 71, Everett Collection, 16, 74, Heritage Images/Ann Ronan Picture Library,
8, Heritage Images/National Motor Museum, 100, Universal Images Group/Dorling Kindersley, 51, ZUMA Press/Top
Gear, 101; Rex by Barry Norman, 108; Science Source: British Dental Association Museum, 102; Shutterstock: Ad Oculos, 50,
alex7370, 109, Andrey_Popov, 103, Arina P Habich, 92-93, arsa35, 56-57, bannosuke, 37 (bottom), belushi, 86, belushi, cover,
(bottom right), Billion Photos, 18, 19, Brad Whitsitt, 52, ensiferum, 12, Everett - Art, 68, , 69, Everett Historical, 2, 66, 104,
Federica Milella, 33, Florin Gabreil, 79, Fouad A. Saad, 13, grocap, 88, HandmadePictures, 60, HodagMedia, 29, iryna1, 7,
itsmejust, 4-5 (all), James Steidl, back cover (all), Javier Brosch, cover, (bottom left), John A Davis, 25, John Kasawa, 30, Juan
Gaertner, 42, 43, Lava 4 images, 26, 27, Lenor Ko, 31, Levent Konuk, 18-19, mariakraynova, 95, Michael Dechev, 49, nexus 7,
84, oneinchpunch, 97, pandapaw, cover, (top right), Pavel L Photo and Video, 10, Pekka Nikonen, 89, prapann, 14-15 (all),
rkafoto, 80, rocharibeiro, 85, Scott Richardson, 75, Suz7, 39, svetajok, 47, Tashatuvango, 58, Thomas M Perkins, 61, tobkatrina,
22, Umberto Shtanzman, 107, vectorEps10, 36, 37 (top), Winston Link, 72, wuzefe, 73, xiaorui, 81, Yomka, 99, zeffir, 34, ziviani,
cover, (top left), 106; SuperStock: DeAgostini, 91, Exactostock/Chris Lyon, 24; Wikimedia: U.S. Air Force, 55

Design Elements by Capstone and Shutterstock